JONAH

A STORY OF REPENTANCE

SAINT **SHENOUDA** PRESS

JONAH

A STORY OF REPENTANCE

ST SHENOUDA PRESS
SYDNEY, AUSTRALIA
2020

Jonah: A Story of Repentance

ST SHENOUDA PRESS
8419 Putty Rd,
Putty, NSW, 2330
Sydney, Australia

www.stshenoudapress.com

ISBN 13: 978-0-6485754-6-7

Cover Design:
Andro Botros

Contents

Introduction

When we face hardships in our lives, we sometimes accuse God that he has forsaken us or that He no longer cares for us. We believe He does not love us because we have gone astray for a while or   have not listened to Him or have abandoned His teachings.

The story of Jonah the prophet is a story that illustrates these do not represent God's true nature. However, all the above misrepresentations are based on either a personal fear of God due to our sins or a misrepresentation of God that Satan has put into our minds when we decide to return to God.

The story of Jonah is a story full of hope for those who have the desire to repent and return to the bosom of God. It is a story that illustrates God's plan for the salvation of every soul, not only those who are already under His Wings, but the ones who are still astray. It displays that God subdues everything and everyone in order to save us.

Jonah the Refugee

The Book of Jonah gives an account of Jonah's refuge and departure from God and His teachings. God tells Jonah: "'Arise, go to Nineveh, that great city, and cry out against it; for their wickedness has come up before Me." But, Jonah arose to flee to Tarshish from the presence of the Lord. He went down to Joppa, and found a ship going to Tarshish. He paid the fare, and went down to go with the crew to Tarshish from the presence of the Lord (Jonah 1:2).

Although Jonah heard God's commandment, he could not carry it out. Jonah's reasons for not implementing God's commandment were different from others. However, the result was the same: the word of God was not obeyed. Often, we listen to sermons, read our Bibles or use other means to communicate with God. Yet, we do not listen to His voice. We even choose to let God's commandments fall on deaf ears and we invent many excuses along the way. In addition to all of this, one thinks that walking with God would stop him from enjoying life to the fullest.

Here we see the beginning of Jonah's journey away from God when he boarded a boat "to go with them to Tarshish from the presence of the Lord" (Jonah 1:3). Jonah thought that if he can flee from the Lord, he would be better off and can enjoy life to the fullest. This is the desire to be free from any meaningful obligations and to break away from anyone or anything that would seem to be stopping them from enjoying life as they see fit. Would God stand still while watching one of His children go astray? Of course not.

Jonah and the Warnings

The Book of Jonah continues: "But the Lord sent out a great wind on the sea, and there was a mighty tempest on the sea, so that the ship was about to be broken up" (Jonah 1:4). Some cars have an automatic braking system that will tell you know how close you are to the car ahead of you, alert you of the danger, and brake automatically to prevent a collision. Once a man's free will begins to drift away from God's will, God starts working on sending various warning messages that escalate in severity. St. John Chrysostom says, "He really escaped from righteousness, but he did not escape the wrath of God! He escaped from the land, but he brought on himself storms in the sea [10]]. It was befitting of him not to escape from God but to God, in which only the believer finds safety and harbor!" Often, we find ourselves drifting away from God, and we do not realize that our safety and well-being are protected by God. Jonah, like all of us, wanted to escape from God's sovereignty and by drifting away from His commandments, he will be safe. Yet, God always has one goal for everyone and that is for "all men to be saved and to come to the knowledge of the truth" (1 Timothy 2:4). If this is the goal, then God begins sending messages to a person going astray hoping for their free will to return them to Him.

An example of a message would be to allow events to occur that shake the ship of our lives (Jonah 1:4) but not enough to break it. Events such as hardships at work, financial difficulties etc, which will not break us. God knows when and where He will interfere, but these are enough to force a person to wake up from the direction they are walking towards. If a person answers God's call, He will either start reversing a situation or provide grace to overcome it.

If a person continues to ignore God's call to Him, God will increase the severity of the situation. In Jonah's case, the disturbance of the sea made the mariners afraid and each of them cried to the god they knew. Jonah himself was oblivious to the events surrounding him. Jonah was "in the lowest parts of the ship, lain down, and was fast asleep" (Jonah 1:5). Jonah was the only one oblivious of what was happening around him and this is exactly what happens when someone moves away from God. They begin losing their spiritual vision, a sense of direction and being. St. Theophan the Recluse describes such a person as: "the sinner who is to be renewed through repentance is often described in the Word of God as being submerged in a deep sleep. The distinctive feature of such person is the absence of an active, heartfelt and selfless desire for pleasing God together with a resolute aversion for everything that is sinful." Often, that person excludes themselves from their surroundings, friends, family, and everyone else because they want to lose all attachments to reality and live in their own self-centered, secluded life. Hence, Jonah was fast asleep. Would God stop at that? No way, He loves Jonah too much to leave him to perish. Hence, God starts to increase the severity of the situation until others, the mariners, started to notice it as well. The mariners start to drop heaving things in the water in case this would help improve the situation. Nothing helped. So they woke Jonah up to pray to his God. They also cast lots "to see for whose cause this trouble has come upon them" (Jonah 1:7). Similarly, for a person who is walking away from God and dealing with hardships, others surrounding them will start feeling these hardships, but they will not be aware of them. Friends and family will begin pointing out issues to them but they will continue to look the other way. Things will get worse and the circle around them starts to close in until, similar to Jonah, they repent and confess that they are running away from God (Jonah 1:8-9). How many times and how often have we found ourselves running away from God willingly and not wanting anything to do with Him because we think that while we are away from Him, we will live a better life? For example, Adam and Eve, decided that they wanted to be equal with God, the One who created them and gave them dominion over creation. Unfortunately, they listened to the serpent and were cast away from the Garden of Eden and the presence of God. They were also abandoned by the devil, who lied to them. God Himself greatly despises sin. A great reminder of this comes when God told Abraham about Sodom and Gomorrah: "And the LORD said, "Because the outcry against Sodom and Gomorrah is great, and because their sin is very grave, I will go down now and see whether they have done altogether according to the outcry against it that has come to Me; and if not, I will know" (Genesis 18:20-21). This is a clear illustration that God not only despises sin, but it annoys Him immensely and views it as an outcry which brings displeasure to Him.

The mariners in the story of Jonah acted in a similar way to Abraham when he reacted to the Lord's proclamation of Sodom and Gomorrah. . Abraham pleaded and interceded on behalf of the people of Sodom saying: "Would You also destroy the righteous with the wicked? Suppose there were fifty righteous within the city; would You also destroy the place and not spare it for the fifty righteous that were in it? Far be it from You to do such a thing as this, to slay the righteous with the wicked, so that the righteous should be as the wicked; far be it from You! Shall not the Judge of all the earth do, right?" (Genesis 18:23-25). Similarly, the mariners had to row hard to return to land, but they could not because God needed them to carry out His plan (Jonah 1:13). They also sought God's mercy and compassion and acknowledged His plan by saying: "We pray, O LORD, please do not let us perish for this man's life, and do not charge us with innocent blood; for You, O LORD, have done as it pleased You"(Jonah 1:14)

St. John Chrysostom describes Jonah's escape and the tempest saying: "Jonah expected to escape by ship, so the ship became constraints to him." God planned to have Jonah surrounded inside a tempest at sea, as well as an unstable ship, to bring him back to repentance. God used the same things Jonah used to escape, such as the sea and the ship to return him to Him once again. St. John Chrysostom continues "There was no need for many days and no continuous advice, but in the simplicity of saying it was the need to be led by everything to repentance (that is, God uses all circumstances to recap). God did not lead him directly from the ship to the city, but he was handed over to the sea, the sea to the fish, the fish to God, and from God to the people of Nineveh, and through this long circle the stray returned until everyone knew that it would not be possible to escape from the hand of God."

The Return to Oneself

Similarly to Jonah, the repentant's road back to God begins when there is the realization that there is no escape from God. Everything that he was planning on utilizing to escape such as the sea and the ship turned against him. This is similar to someone who tried to escape from God through befriending others and trying to do some handy work to receive money. God closes that circle on a person by allowing fights to break out between friends and allow managers to realize that this person is not responsible enough which creates an uncomfortable work environment and a possibility to become unemployed. A person would finally end up realizing that everything that they were chasing was nothing but a mirage and once they answer that call, they find themselves alone and losing everything including themselves. Jonah came to this conclusion. He realized that everything that he hoped for was being used against him to the point that he knew that the only way to calm the sea was for the mariners to throw him into it. St. John Chrysostom comments: "The city was disturbed by the sins of the people of Nineveh, and the ship was disturbed by the Prophet's disobedience. So, the sailors threw Jonah into the deep sea and the ship was preserved. Let's also throw our sins, so our city remains safe and secure." St. John Chrysostom makes the connection that the disturbance which the unrepentant deals with in their life is due to their disobedience towards God. In this case, why would the unrepentant remain in their path, if they know that all of this is happening because of their disobedience towards God's commandments? Those who have gone astray for a very long time may not realize the reason but once they do, they will likely become worried that God will not accept their return. They may fear returning to their families, their earlier life, their church, and their communities due to their previous reputation and the accusing looks they will receive from others. This should never be the case.

Now that Jonah had confessed his desire to escape from God, he commanded the mariners to throw him in the sea in order to be tamed. St. Jerome indicates that the action of tossing Jonah into the sea is a prophecy about the suffering of our Lord Jesus Christ. Through His death, the tempest of our world was removed and He saved the ship of our life. Through the suffering of our Lord Jesus Christ, the world was filled with great inner peace.

Similarly, St. Paul in his letter to the Philippians says: "that I may know Him and the power of His resurrection, and the fellowship of His sufferings, being conformed to His death, if by any means, I may attain to the resurrection from the dead" (Philippians 3:10). Therefore, if St. Paul is indicating that we should have fellowship with Christ in His suffering and that the tossing of Jonah in the sea was a prophecy about His suffering, it is befitting to think that since we have accepted to be called children of God that we should throw our old man with his deeds, our old Jonah, behind us and obtain the new Jonah with his new deeds that are acceptable to God (Galatians 3:27). We should not only put on Christ but also remember that since we have received the Sacrament of Baptism that we are now hidden in Christ (Galatians 3:27) and hence, "He (Christ) must increase, but I must decrease." (St. John 3:30). Therefore, on the path to repentance, one must think about where they went astray in their actions and correct them while increasing the work of God in their lives.

The Repented Soul

Once Jonah was thrown into the sea, "the Lord had prepared a great fish to swallow Jonah. And Jonah was in the belly of the fish three days and three nights." (Jonah 1:17) During that time, Jonah came back to himself and started praying to God for mercy and repenting for his actions. This is an example of a true repentant soul. Additionally, sometimes God forces us into solitude to obtain this kind of spiritual benefit and allows us to benefit from looking inwards at ourselves and examining how we appear to Him. This inner examination is far more beneficial than the words of praise one receives from people. As the Bible says: "for what man knows the things of a man except the spirit of the man which is in him?" (1 Corinthians 2) Hence, it is desirable for a person to examine their inner self rather than accept this praise from those who do not know them well lest their path to eternal life is hindered through their egotistical view of themselves.

Once the Jonah that is in each one of us starts to calm down and become focused, he will start seeing his life and his relationship with Him through different lenses. Often when he is silenced, he will start hearing God's voice which is normally in the form of whispers. In order to hear His voice, we need to be looking inside of ourselves to watch where we are heading spiritually and to correct our course accordingly.

Jonah was forced to calm down in the belly of the fish. Inside, Jonah was trapped in a grave, where his thoughts, abilities and possibilities died and he did not know what to do. He could not expect what would happen to him. Only then did Jonah begin to turn to the One who can help him when everyone else has failed. He is in a grave-like belly, his friends and family are far away, and no one can know which fish to capture if they even wanted to save him. The only one that knows where he is, can help capture that fish and is able to command it to drop him off at the shore is God. This is exactly what often happens to us. We feel that we are trapped, closed in, and helpless and we suddenly remember God and turn to Him. This is the largest step to repentance, which is seeking God, not only to get us out of the fish, but to always be with Him for the rest of our lives.

Once Jonah realized he had to turn to God, he prays "to the Lord his God from the fish's belly." (Jonah 2:1). When Jonah turns his heart towards God, the Bible emphasizes this with "his God." Yet, when Jonah is questioned by the mariners about who he was, he mentioned that: "I fear the Lord, the God of heaven, who made the sea and the dry land." (Jonah 1:9). When the old Jonah was going astray, God seemed to be very far away and is described as "the God of heaven." However, when the repentant, new Jonah is changing his ways to return to God, He is now called "His God." Therefore, God is always in the same position, yet we are the ones that either move closer or further from Him. His relation to us changes based on where we are positioned in relation to Him. Hence, Jonah prayed to God even though he was the one that tried to run away from Him. How would God react to the prayer of one who did not obey him, but now needs His help? Would God listen to Jonah's prayer?

The True Repentance

When Jonah found himself helpless, on his own, not knowing what to do, he did what many of us lack the courage to do: he prayed to God. Many sinners believe that God will not take them back nor hear their prayers when they want to return. Sometimes, sinners think that they have done many bad things that God will never listen to their prayers or hear them out. On the contrary, St. John Chrysostom says about the prayer of Jonah: "let us not worry about the place but the Lord of the place, Jonah was in the belly of the fish and God heard his prayer. Even if you were in places where no one would hear you pray. Anywhere and everywhere you are praying and do not ask for the place where you will pray in because your soul is the temple." However, what makes Jonah unique and a minority in how he felt about praying to God is that he had a very strong faith in God's mercy. Before God answers his prayers, Jonah says, "I cried out to the Lord because of my affliction, and He answered me" (Jonah 2:2). Jonah had such a strong faith that God did not only listen to his prayers but answered them as well. Jonah goes on to say that "out of the belly of Sheol I cried, and You heard my voice" (Jonah2:2).

 Again, here we see how Jonah does not only know that God will hear him, but Jonah is conversing with God as if He, God, is already talking back to him. A truly repenting person would not only pray to God with faith, but they would have the desire to start a long-awaited conversation with the One they desire. The repentant, like Jonah, would realize that the one who allowed these hardships to happen is God (Jonah 2:3). That person would finally realize that they have been cast out of the sight of the Lord (Jonah 2:4) and because they left God, the grace of God left them making them vulnerable to all the hardships. This is the moment that God is waiting for, the return of His children to His Fatherly bosom. God is the source of all love, and as in the story of the prodigal son, the Father was waiting outside of His palace anxious for His son's return to Him. God does the same. He does not wait in His palace which is in Heaven, but He waits outside closer to the person waiting for his return. Therefore, we should not misunderstand why we are faced with hardships since they can sometimes be the way to get us back on track in order to realize that we are being led astray from God. Jonah's hope in God was extremely strong to the point that he forgot that he was in the belly of a fish and in his conversation with God, he is already aware of God's mercy covering the multitude of his sins and that he will return and look again toward the temple of the Lord (Jonah 2:4). We can learn from Jonah that God never turns down those who turn to Him. St. James says: "Draw near to God and He will draw near to you. Cleanse your hands, you sinners; and purify your hearts, you double-minded" (St. James 4:8). Therefore, God accepts the repentant, the one who also confesses and agrees not to return to where he was once before. Here Jonah illustrates clearly what he learned from his previous relationship with God; that He never turns away a person who is truly repent no matter how severe his sin is or how long he has been away from Him.

God always awaits the problem with us. Jonah, like many, says "when my soul fainted within me, I remembered the Lord" (Jonah 2:7). It means that when all else has failed to resolve an issue, we turn to God. As humans, we ask a series of famous questions when people turn to us for help especially when they have turned to others for help before us. For example: why are you asking me? Why now? When Jonah lost all hope in human support, only then does he remember the Lord and turns to Him for help. What would God do in return for this call for help? Would He answer Jonah's prayers? Would He rebuke him for not obeying Him? Would He leave him for a while wondering what He would do so he would learn his lesson?

The Fruits of Repentance

God is not like humans. He never holds grudges against anyone. He never rebukes anyone who is coming back to Him but He receives them with open arms. God is the infinite source of love, kindness, and fatherhood, among other things. Hence, when dealing with Jonah, He did not rebuke him for what he had done, He did not let his prayers fall on deaf ears, and He did not leave him for a while to learn His lesson. God immediately responded to the truthful prayer of repentance that came from Jonah's heart, because "the righteous God tests the hearts and the minds" (Psalm 7:9). God "spoke to the fish and it vomited Jonah onto dry land." (Jonah 2:10). Was this the complex issue that Jonah was dealing with? Was it the issue that made his soul faint within him? Yes, indeed it was the very complex issue that seemed unsolvable to Jonah and he spent three days trying to figure out a solution then finally cried out to God. What seemed to be a very complex issue to Jonah was resolved with a single command to the fish. God is the Almighty and Pantocrator who has power and authority over the heaven and earth and over all things in between the two, including human emotions.

Now that God had solved Jonah's problem, He again asked him to carry out the spiritual task that He had originally given to him, which was to go into the city of Nineveh and send them a message from God. Here, God illustrated that He immediately reinstates a person's relationship and status with Him. He reinstated Jonah as a prophet again and commanded him to carry a message to the city of Nineveh. In addition, God solves our immediate earthly needs, like Jonah's, so we can focus on carrying out the spiritual needs of our journey to heaven. God, in answering our earthly needs, hopes that we would focus on the heavenly shortfalls that we have. However, sometimes, our reception of this goal is not clear, similar to those who searched for our Lord Jesus Christ after the miracle of the five loaves and two fishes and He told them: "you are not seeking me because of the miracles I have performed but because you have eaten the loves and you were filled" (St. John 6:22-40). Here again we see another shortfall of mankind illustrated in the life of Jonah. Nineveh was a great city, a three-day journey in size, however, Jonah did not preach in all of it He only preached a day's worth and delivered God's message that in forty days the city shall be overthrown (Jonah 4:3-4). The shortfall is that

Jonah did not complete the full spiritual task that was commanded by God; he only completed one-third of it. Yet, we see that God picks up his shortfall and his slack attitude and completes the message so it arrives to all of Nineveh including the king. God does the same with the repenting person. He is always right there to help the repentant through His grace and completes every spiritual shortfall that we have. God only asks that our will aligns with His: "and in the wilderness where you saw how the LORD your God carried you, as a man carries his son, in all the way that you went until you came to this place" (Deuteronomy 1:31). Hence, through our journey to repentance, God is the one who carries us and covers our short falls along the way. All He desires from us is to align our will with His and that we have a desire to inherit eternal life.

Finally, it is apparent at the end how God thinks in regards to the sinful who needs repentance: "you have pity on the plant for which you have not labored, nor made it grow, which came up in a night and perished in a night. And should I not pity Nineveh, that great city, in which are more than one hundred and twenty thousand persons who cannot discern between their right hand and their left- and much livestock?" (Jonah 4:10) Hence, we can see God's extreme care for the sinful to repent and for those who are astray to return.

No matter where we are in our repentant life, each one

of us has an old Jonah in us that we need to get rid of in order to align ourselves to God's will. No matter how long we have been astray from God, He is always there to carry us through if we allow Him to do so. If God Himself is with us, who can be against us? How people look at us throughout our journey towards repentance is not important but the most important thing is where I am in my relationship with God. St. Paul says: "for whom I have suffered the loss of all things, and count them as rubbish, that I may gain Christ and be found in Him" (Philippians 3:8-9). Therefore, nothing in life can be compared to gaining a strong relationship with God on earth that will continue to eternity. Additionally, we should not be overwhelmed with troubles of this world because no matter how complex the matter is, God is the only one who will be able to help us resolve it with a single word. Also, remember the words of St. John Chrysostom regarding repentance: "do not be ashamed to enter again into the church. Be ashamed when you sin. Do not be ashamed when you repent. Pay attention to what the devil did to you. These are two things: sin and repentance. Sin is a wound; repentance is a medicine. Just as there are for the body wounds and medicines, so for the soul are sins and repentance. However, sin has the shame and repentance possesses the courage." Hence, nothing is shameful about returning but it is a devilish trick to keep us away from God's bosom. We should make the effort and have the zeal and desire to return and let God be our Protector along the way.

Prayers of the Early Church Fathers for Repentance.

St. Jerome: "O Good Shepherd, seek me out, and bring me home to Thy fold again. Deal favorably with me according to Thy good pleasure, till I may dwell in Thy house all the days of my life and praise Thee for ever and ever with them that are there."

St. Clement of Rome: "We beseech Thee, Master, to be our Helper and Protector. Save the afflicted among us; have mercy on the lowly; raise up the fallen; appear to the needy; heal the ungodly; restore the wanderers of Thy people; feed the hungry; ransom our prisoners; raise up the sick; comfort the faint-hearted."

St. Jerome: "Lord, thou hast given us Thy Word for a light to shine upon our path; grant us so to meditate on that Word, and to follow its teaching, that we may find in it the light that shines more and more until the perfect day; through Jesus Christ our Lord."

St. Basil the Great: "As I rise from sleep I thank Thee, O Holy Trinity, for through Thy great goodness and patience Thou wast not angered with me, an idler and sinner, nor hast Thou destroyed me in my sins, but hast shown Thy usual love for men, and when I was prostrate in despair, Thou hast raised me to keep the morning watch and glorify Thy power. And now enlighten my mind's eye and open my mouth to study Thy words and understand Thy commandments and do Thy will and sing to Thee in heartfelt adoration and praise Thy Most Holy Name of Father, Son and Holy Spirit, now and ever, and to the ages of ages. Amen